WORKSPACE WONDERS

CREATING A WORKSPACE

THAT WORKS FOR YOU!

Caroline R. Bailey

Transform Your Workspace to Increase Your Productivity & Income Utilizing the Power of Lean Six Sigma

Copyright © 2016 by Caroline R. Bailey
All rights reserved.

This workbook is dedicated in loving memory to my Mentor and dearest Friend

Paul H. Huey

1939-2015

Thank you, Paul, for believing in me even when I didn't believe in myself.

I love you and miss you so much, Sweet Friend – until we meet again!

Dear Reader,

If I came to visit you right now, this very instant, in your workspace, would I see you reflected in it?

Is your workspace a mirror reflection of who you are, what you do, what you believe in, work for, and strive for?

Is your workspace really working for you or are you working for your workspace?

In this workbook, we are going to take a hard look at your daily processes and procedures, your workspaces, and your time management.

We will learn to use the tools of Lean Six Sigma to transform your workspace into dignified, empowering spaces, with processes and procedures that build self-worth and business profit at the same time.

So, what is Lean Six Sigma?

Lean Six Sigma is a combination of two separate business methodologies blended together as a structured approach for problem solving and process optimization.

Lean concentrates on improving process flow, and Six Sigma concentrates on high quality.

Lean Six Sigma results in the highest level of quality in the shortest amount of time possible for the process.

By implementing Lean Six Sigma concepts, organizations can change for the better.

I was drawn to Lean Six Sigma because as an office manager and a single mother, I wanted to work smarter and not harder. I needed more time for my Daughter, and more time for myself...

Once I enrolled in the program, I began to realize that Lean Six Sigma can be applied to completely overhaul antiquated systems and streamline processes and procedures. It saves time and money!

Now I teach and prove that organizations can change for the better. It is my mission, my Divine responsibility, my passion – to take the concepts that I have learned and practice to teach, show, lead, and guide others.

Lean Six Sigma can be used by anyone at anytime in their homes, farms, classrooms, boardrooms, workspaces, assembly lines, organizations, or corporations.

Lean Six Sigma can increase productivity, increase quality, and increase income.

My goal is to help you see and then experience the possibility of greatness within your processes, yourselves, and your workspaces.

Blessings to you as begin your transformation,
Caroline

So, what is Lean Six Sigma?

Lean Six Sigma is a combination of Lean and Six Sigma which are business initiatives that are based on improving performance in a process by using specific tools and statistical techniques.

Lean Six Sigma leads us to adopt a mindset and a work style in which we are seeking Continuous Improvement.

You are constantly looking and reviewing and tweaking all of your processes – always wanting to aim for that smooth running machine, a well-oiled machine, so to speak.

Lean Six Sigma

Lean Six Sigma is a combination of two separate business methodologies blended together as a structured approach for problem solving and process optimization.

So let's take a look at each individually to get a better grasp on how you can use Lean Six Sigma to your advantage.

LEAN HELPS YOU MAKE IT FASTER!

Lean is all about improving your process flow, reducing process complexity – it wants to simplify, reduce waste, and create value.

Lean is all about improving your process so it runs faster.

Lean wants you to be a detective and ask yourself:

- Can this process be streamlined?
- Can this be improved?
- Do I really need to do this?

Lean guides you to really look at your current process and see where you can take your time back and where you can reduce waste along the way.

Six Sigma helps you make it better!

So what is Six Sigma?

Now, Six Sigma is a statistic that is a measure of the number of defects in a specific process or operation.

Six Sigma is a statistical measure of Quasi Perfection – which states that a process must not produce more than 3.4 defects per million opportunities which is 99.9997% perfect – almost practically perfect!

Six Sigma is all about reducing process variation, it reduces defects, and drives quality, and again, it strives for near perfection - That is why I like to think about Ivory Soap!

Ivory Soap states that it is 99.994% pure - and you want a pure process, too, a practically perfect process!

You want to clean up your process, make your process better, and once you get your process as close to perfect as possible, you want to put in control measures to keep it that way.

Why Lean Six Sigma?

So when you blend Lean and Six Sigma together you are working to:

- reduce waste
- reduce non value added work
- reduce time
- improve quality
- improve cost

You can begin implementing and transforming your traditional operations to Lean Six Sigma to make all of your processes faster and better.

You can take back your time and you can reduce defects or errors because defects and errors cost money.

Lean Six Sigma gives you tools to tweak a process so you get the same quality at the same speed every single time because Lean Six Sigma eliminates variation in your process.

VARIATION IS NOT YOUR FRIEND!

Again, Lean Six Sigma is all about eliminating variation in a process. Your goal is to eliminate variation. So why do we want to do that?

Well, as a customer the worst experience I can imagine is being the casualty of process variation!

If it doesn't seem that bad to you right now, just think back for a second and see if any of this has happened to you:

- o You went to the Grocery Store only to select the slowest checkout in the store

- You got a haircut but it was shorter than usual and not what you asked for
- You got your hair colored and it was a shade too light or too dark
- Or you ordered your steak medium-well and it came out rare

Now I am sure that you can probably come up with a list of your own experiences like this, but you can also come up with times that you got through the store lighting fast, got a perfect cut or color, and when your steak was perfectly delicious.

That is a great feeling isn't it? That is what you want all the time.

Lean Six Sigma can do that for you.

You can use it to gain a stronger understanding of your processes, to achieve a level of quality that satisfies your customer and minimizes losses of your time and your money.

Why Lean Six Sigma?

Why Lean Six Sigma?

LEAN SIX SIGMA
HELPS YOU SOLVE
PROBLEMS!

Again, you can begin implementing and transforming your traditional process to Lean Six Sigma to make all of your processes faster and better.

You can take back your time and you can reduce defects or errors and you can save money.

So I am going to give you a few simple Lean Six Sigma tools to get you started!

Remember in the Disney movie, *Mary Poppins*, when Mary Poppins sang "In every job that must be done there is an element of fun? Find the fun and snap, the job's a game!"

Well, that is what you are going to do with Lean Six Sigma so let's first take a look at problem solving.

PROBLEM SOLVING USING LEAN SIX SIGMA

Element of Discovery!

But let me start off saying right now - do not get overwhelmed!!

One thing that I love about Lean Six Sigma is that when you really start to investigate your processes and your work spaces, there is this element of surprise to it – something that seemingly comes out of nowhere –

WHAM!!

– Here is the issue I need to fix, this is where my problem is– and that is what makes it fun!

From Christopher Columbus to Lewis and Clark to little folks at an Easter egg hunt – we all love that element of discovery, so let's have fun with it, okay?

WHERE IS MY PROBLEM?

Houston, We have a Problem...

Okay, so problems are really a problem, right?

So, what is a problem?

The Concise Oxford Dictionary defines a problem as:

"A doubtful or difficult matter requiring a solution" and also as "Something hard to understand or accomplish or deal with"

But I want to give you a simpler definition that my Teacher taught me:

A problem is simply the difference between what is and what should be.

Again:

A problem is the difference between what is and what should be.

Problem solving is a key skill, and it's one that can make a huge difference in your life.

At work, problems are at the center of what many people do every day – like you are constantly putting out fires.

You're either solving a problem for a client, or helping someone who is solving a problem, or discovering new problems to solve.

And these problems you face can be large or small, simple or complex, and easy or difficult to solve.

Let's try a simple exercise – Brainstorming!

I want you to write out at least 5 things about your personal space of income generation that you think are holding you back on a financial or personal level:

A problem is the difference between what is and what should be.

What Is: **_What Should Be:_**

So now that we have your list, let's move forward!

Regardless of the nature of the problems, the most fundamental part of your role is finding ways to solve them.

So, being a confident problem solver is really important to your success. And much of that confidence comes from having a good process to use when approaching a problem.

With a really good process, you can solve problems quickly and effectively.

Without a really good process, your solutions may be ineffective, or you'll get stuck and do nothing, and sometimes with painful consequences.

And you can use a Lean Six Sigma tool – a tool called the DMAIC method to solve problems.

The DMAIC Method

DMAIC is an acronym for five interconnected phases which refer to Define, Measure, Analyze, Improve, and Control.

The DMAIC method helps us to achieve the highest level of perfection possible in the business environments in which you operate.

It is made up of 5 separate phases, which start off with a Define phase, then move on to a Measure phase, then move on to an Analyze phase, and then to the Improve phase, and then to the final phase, the Control phase.

DMAIC Helps Solve problems...
- Define opportunity
- Measure Performance
- Analyze Opportunity
- Improve Performance
- Control Performance

DMAIC HELPS SOLVE PROBLEMS

Each phase in the DMAIC Process is required to ensure the best possible results.

The DMAIC helps us to:

Define the problem and the process involved.

Then you measure the performance of the process involved.

Next you analyze the data collected and map out your process to determine root causes of defects or errors and opportunities for improvement.

Then you want to improve the process by designing creative solutions to fix and prevent problems.

Finally you want to control the improvements to keep the process on the new course.

DEFINE YOUR PROBLEM

You begin the DMAIC by asking yourself some questions.

You know, it is so important to question everything so you can grow and you can learn - but the thing about questions is that –

If you do not ask the right questions you will not get the right answers!

Define your problem

- Root Cause Analysis is a useful process for understanding and solving a problem.

- As an analytical tool, Root Cause Analysis is an essential way to perform a comprehensive, system-wide review of significant problems as well as the events and factors leading to them.

The thing that I love about Lean Six Sigma is that it uses the simplest tools to change things in big ways.

Lean Six Sigma has a super simple tool called 5 Whys.

You just ask why 5 times. Just like little children do!

You can use 5 whys to drill down into any problem. So let's try it out.

FINDING YOUR ROOT CAUSE

Root Cause: 5 WHYS

Why? → Why? → Why? → Why? → Why? – Root Cause

Let's take a look at an example to see the easy magic of the 5 Whys...

Find Your root cause with the 5 Whys

I have a problem with a prospective client. He seems to be avoiding me for some reason.

So I write it down and then I ask myself

Why?

Well, because I think he is displeased with me or something – I don't know.

Well Why?

Because I had to cancel your initial Skype call that I had set up.

Why?

Because I had my Daughter's school event the same day and had to be there then.

Well Why?

Because I forgot to email to reschedule the meeting so I had to just cancel at the last minute

Why?

Because I got distracted - the dog was barking and I went to check to see what was going on.

See how easy this is?

We started with a problem and now we know exactly what we need to work on – the 5whys helped me get to the possible root causes of my issues and now I know that I need to work on distractions and I need to work on how to keep up with things better.

And I might even need to check into Doggy Day Care...

So let's go back to your Problem List and try it out!

A problem is the difference between what is and what should be.

	What Is:	*What Should Be:*
#1		
#2		
#3		
#4		
#5		

Now, start with whichever problem you want and begin to ask yourself WHY?

5 Whys

What Is:

What Should Be:

Why?

Why?

Why?

Why?

Why?

Goal Setting

So now you can use the 5 whys and then you know your root cause of your problem, and you can go about solving it.

Your goal is to solve that problem.

Let's take a little time to work smarter and not harder, so let's set up SMART goals!

SMART goals are:

- **S**pecific
- **M**easurable
- **A**chievable
- **R**elevant
- **T**imely

So let's delve into a goal or two and make sure that they are SMART!

Specific: *What exactly will I accomplish?*

Measurable: *How will I know when I have reached my goal?*

Achievable: *Can my goal be achieved with my effort and my commitment?*

Relevant: *Why is this goal significant to me?*

Timely: *When will I achieve this goal?*

The outward transformation really begins with an inner transformation – let's take some time to focus in on your goals and work smarter and not harder at achieving them...

Points to Ponder...

☐ Why is this goal important to me?

☐ What are the benefits of my achieving of this goal?

☐ What steps do I need to take to achieve my goal?

☐ Do I need to ask anyone to help me? If so, who?

And now that you have a clearly defined problem and a goal to solve that problem, you can use tools in the Measure and Analyze Phase of the DMAIC method to help you further investigate your problem.

The best tools you will want to use to really look at your process and the problems in it are Process Flow Maps and Value Streams Maps.

MEASURE AND ANALYZE

Measure & analyze

- Process Flow Charts and Value Stream Maps are used to document, analyze and improve the flow of information or materials required to produce a product or service.
- We look at all our Inputs and our Outputs!
- Opportunities for improvement can be found anywhere in or along the flow of the process!

Process maps and value stream maps are designed to **capture the value** of each activity and the impact it has.

With this information, you can work to reduce or remove the activities that are not adding value and improve upon activities that do—reducing costs while increasing the value of your process.

You are going to chart out every single step in your process and really look at it to identify sources of variation and to identify gaps between current performance and goal performance, and prioritize opportunities to improve.

So let's start with something I dearly love – Peanut Butter and Jelly Sandwiches! Yum!

PB & J Process Map

```
Get Bread out of    →  Get Peanut Butter   →  Get a plate out of  →  Get Jelly out of the
Pantry                 out of the Cabinet     cabinet                Fridge
                                                                         ↓
Open the jar of     ←  Place bread slice on ←  Open bread and     ←  Get a knife out of
peanut butter          the plate              remove two slices      the drawer
    ↓
Take knife and      →  Flip the top of the  →  Put slices of bread →  Use knife to cut
spread peanut          jelly and squirt on     together on plate      sandwich in half
butter on one slice    the other slice of
of bread               bread
                                                                         ↓
Take sandwhich on   ←  Close bread bag and  ←  Close the lid on   ←  Put knife in the sink
plate to table to eat  place back in pantry    jetlly and place back
                                               in the fridge
```

In your PB & J Process Map, you can easily see your inputs and outputs right along the way.

Now, the process of making your sandwich - that is where we write down every single activity, no matter how small, and we place that in a little box along your process path so we can determine if the particular step or activity is value added, non value added, which is waste, and also begin to think about reducing variation in it.

Again, process maps and value stream maps are designed to evaluate each activity and the impact it has.

You are going to chart out every single step in your process and really look at it to get rid of waste and variation so we are doing the same thing in the same time frame with the same level of quality.

So now it's your turn! Pick out one of your daily processes and make yourself a Map!

MY PROCESS MAP

```
[Starting Point] → [ ] → [ ] → [ ]
                                 ↓
[ ] ← [ ] ← [ ] ← [ ]
  ↓
[ ] → [ ] → [Ending Point]
```

We want to make your process a natural flow of perfection, and we want to make sure your process is pure and unobstructed.

You can use these process flow charts and value stream maps ask yourself three questions that are super important to taking back your time and saving you money – we want to determine two things with each step in your process:

We want to know if your work is **value added** or is your work **non-value added** or **waste**?

Value stream mapping

Don't Poison Your Stream!

Think of your process like a stream – where does it start and where does it end? Is it fast or are there obstructions that slow it down?

These obstructions or the things that slow us down – this where you want to really focus on to take out time back.

So think about your daily activities for a second - value adding activities do as the name suggests, "add value" it is anything you do to transform materials or information into something that your process or your clients require.

Non Value Adding activities can be a bit tricky, as this is something that consumes resources, and does not create any value for the client, but is still currently necessary to supply the service, and waste is definitely non value adding.

A waste is any activity that consumes resources, but does not create any value for the client.

For example, a value added activity might be for you that you are emailing out invoices to clients that have email.

A non-value added activity might be you having to actually mail the invoice to a client because they do not have their email address.

A waste might be you having to walk across the room to go get a stamp and envelope in order to mail it.

So, how do we determine which steps or activities in your process are

- Value Added Tasks
- Non Value Added Tasks
- Waste

Let's make a handy dandy chart!

VALUE ADDED VS. NON VALUE ADDED CHART

Your chart is a super simple tool to help you organize and pinpoint exactly where we can streamline, reduce waste, and reduce variation. It looks like this:

	Value Added	Non Value Added
Necessary	Continuous Improvement	Eliminate if Possible
Unnecessary	Eliminate if Possible	Eliminate Immediately

So you can use Lean Six Sigma to think about ideas to eliminate the wasteful and necessary non vale adding activities and ways to implement those ideas.

Now you are looking at your process as a flow, as a stream, and you can take your process map your value stream map and look at each step and ask yourself is this step value added, or a necessary non value added step, or is it just a waste?

You can categorize these activities into one of the three and list it off to the side on your value stream map as a value added, or a necessary non value added, or a waste.

Then you can begin to think about ideas to eliminate the wasteful and possibly the necessary non vale adding activities.

Then you can begin to implement your ideas to see what works and what doesn't.

Let's try it out with your PB & J Process! Here is your Map...

```
[Get Bread out of Pantry] → [Get Peanut Butter out of the Cabinet] → [Get a plate out of cabinet] → [Get Jelly out of the Fridge]
                                                                                                              ↓
[Open the jar of peanut butter] ← [Place bread slice on the plate] ← [Open bread and remove two slices] ← [Get a knife out of the drawer]
        ↓
[Take knife and spread peanut butter on one slice of bread] → [Flip the top of the jelly and squirt on the other slice of bread] → [Put slices of bread together on plate] → [Use knife to cut sandwhich in half]
                                                                                                                                                ↓
[Take sandwhich on plate to table to eat] ← [Close bread bag and place back in pantry] ← [Close the lid on jetlly and place back in the fridge] ← [Put knife in the sink]
```

And here is your VA vs. NVA Chart…

	Value Added	**Non Value Added**
Necessary	Bread Peanut Butter Jelly	Knife Plate
Unnecessary	Knife Plate Gathering Items	Can I keep items together to reduce the travel, maybe?

So now it is your turn!

Take a look at your process map and begin to fill in your Value Added vs. Non Value Added Chart...

MY VALUE ADDED VS. NON VALUE ADDED CHART

	Value Added	Non Value Added
Necessary		
Unnecessary		

Great job!

So now that you have examined your daily processes, let's take a look at where you are performing those daily activities: your workspace!

Workspace Woes

What if your problem is your workspace?

Wonder if you start working through the 5 whys and mapping out your process and reviewing your value added and non value added activities and you find that your work space is running you and not you running the workspace?

Then you have a real problem in that your workspace is working against you and stealing time from you.

Again, your workspace is working against you and is stealing your time, your energy, your money away from you.

You might not have realized that your workspace is actually stressing you out and this discovery is really huge for us!

So let's use Lean Six Sigma to really look at your workspace and see who the boss of whom is –

We want your spaces to work for us - we are in control.

You need your spaces to give you what you need when you need it in order to do what you need to do when you need to do it!

Points to Ponder…

☐ Where is your workspace?

☐ What do you like about your workspace?

☐ What do you dislike about your workspace?

☐ Do you feel like this space is yours?

☐ Do you think that your workspace reflects who you are?

☐ What do you want to change about your workspace?

Improve and Control

So if your work space is working against you, you can use tools in the Improve and Control Phase of the DMAIC method to take your personal power back.

I love Lean Six Sigma because it utilizes such simple tools, and one of my favorites is a tool called 5S, which is based on Japanese housekeeping!

5S is Japanese housekeeping terminology used in Lean Six Sigma with the Japanese words *seiri, seiton, seiso, seiketsu, and shitsuke.*

So 5S is the method in which Japanese parents taught their children housekeeping!

The 5 S in Japanese Housekeeping stand for:

- ☐ ***Sort***
- ☐ ***Set in Order***
- ☐ ***Shine***
- ☐ ***Standardize***
- ☐ ***Sustain***

I will go through each one of these and give you a rule and a question to ask yourself so you can use it, okay?

Sort

All right, so the first S is Sort.

Your rule here is when in doubt, move it out!

And your question to ask yourselves is:

Do I use this day in and day out?

You want to keep only essential items around us and in your space.

Sort: When in Doubt move it out!

Sort: When In doubt, move it Out!

Sort into piles!

Take Everything Out!

http://images.viralnova.com/000/043/032/office-supplies.png
http://nebula.wsimg.com/c357449f2c51e69ccc61b2acd1bfc5d4?AccessKeyId=68BEDB2E77BB5FC3DECA&disposition=0&alloworigin=1

Keep only the things that you actually use to do your job and get rid of everything you do not use – you need to remove it from the area.

So you want to take everything out and make two piles – a "To Keep" pile and a "To Go" pile. That is all you want to do for right now – just sort in two piles keep or go and that is it.

For right now, just sit a box beside you and put stuff in there that you do not use in the "To Go" box. If it is piece of furniture or a piece of equipment and you cannot move it yourself, and then ask to have it moved.

Again, we only want those items that you actually use day in and day out in your workspace – everything else has to go - and do not start in with any type of judgments or decisions at this point, the items in the "To Go" box are just not needed in your space, and it just needs a new home.

And the new home could be somewhere else in the house or in a new workspace somewhere else – we are not concerned with that at the moment, and we will do all that later, okay?

For now, just make two piles, a "To Keep" pile and a "To Go" pile.

Now as for the items that you will keep, here you want to use a rule of thumb I call the Perfect 10. So think of Perfect 10 – the best of the best, the crème de la crème, and the top dog. If it is not a Perfect 10 then get it out of there!

Put it in the "To Go" box or have it removed from your space – I know this might sound harsh, but items that are not 100% what you need actually hurt you and do not help you.

Now, back to the "To Go" pile - the "To Go" box will need to just sit there for a bit while you sort. Then, I suggest that you stick it in a closet or an area outside of your workspace for at least two weeks.

Within the next two weeks, if you do not have to go to the "To Go" box and get something back out, and then it is meant for a new home, okay?

And when thinking of a new home for these items you removed and put in the to-go box, think about with whom can I gift this with?

- ☐ My child's school?
- ☐ A local shelter?
- ☐ Or a Non Profit?
- ☐ Do I have a friend I can swap out this out with for something else?

So now that you have your things sorted out by what stays and what goes, you can move on to your second S – set in order.

SET IN ORDER!

The second S is set in Order.

Your rule here is a place for everything and everything in its place.

Your question to ask is

Where do I need to put this so I can get to it the quickest?

Here you want to really look at your natural habits.

Your space must reflect exactly what you need it to do for you and not anybody else.

Where do you like to do things?

Again, put things where they are most natural for you and your movements in that space.

Set in order: a place for everything and everything in its place!

SET IN ORDER: A PLACE FOR EVERYTHING AND EVERYTHING IN ITS PLACE

So we go back to your keep pile from your things that we sorted and we decided where the best place for this item is.

Again, where can I get to this item the quickest and easiest?

Where does my hand naturally move towards to reach for something?

Here we want easy access and to what we use the most. You want to keep items in the same spot all the time so you can go right to it when you need it.

You want dedicated storage areas to automatically keep items in orderly fashion, where every single item or groups of items all have their own special spots, there little homes, so they can be right there to help you when you need them to help.

And as you are setting your new space, your new work house in order, this is a great time to be thankful and appreciative of what you have and what you do, and how things like your phone, and computer, and sticky notes support you and help you earn an income to support your lifestyle.

Think of them as tools of the trade and as little employees that help you make money and that have their own little jobs.

This is also a good time to make an inventory list and inspect things for safety and see what needs to be replaced but don't do anything with the list yet, you will get to that later.

If you need new pens, just that down for now, but don't do anything just yet, okay?

See how you are making your space work for you?

And again, your workspace wants to do that, it wants to serve you, to fulfill its purpose in your life.

Let it do what it is supposed to do.

So now that you have sorted and set things in order you can move on to the 3rd S which is shine.

Shine

So, the 3rd S is Shine.

Your rule here is to be clean is to be Lean!

And your question is

How quickly can I get this back in its place?

All through college I was a preschool teacher, and I loved it - it was my favorite job. In your classrooms we had zones, and we had clean up time.

We sang a clean-up song and made it a game and we had the entire room cleaned up and everything back in place by the time we finished singing the song.

SHINE – TO BE LEAN IS TO BE CLEAN

Shine: To be clean is to be lean!

So in your space you want the same thing, here you want to clean up as you go, and make sure that each of your items, your employees are back in the space they are meant to be so when you need them to report to duty they are right there.

And here too in Shine is where we want to clean up – vacuum, dust, straighten up your shelves and use a can of air to blow the dust off your keyboard and all your cords and things.

But I want to make sure that I am crystal clear on this point – this is not just cleaning as in cleaning up a messy room.

Yes, it might be dusty and a bit messy but I am not saying your problem is that you are messy – it is not that.

It is not about mess, it is about a system.

You have no time whatsoever to be tracking down a lost item and you do not have the time for a pity party for the blame game of I am just messy or unorganized, or whatever.

It is not about messiness, or self-blame; it is about your space giving and adding to your energy not taking energy away.

Shine is about self-care, and a neat, streamlined area is easy on the eyes and supports you.

It reduces stress and instantly brings dignity to your workspace and automatically helps you save time and take care of yourself.

Again, think of your value stream map, we want a space that is natural and aligned with your natural movements, okay?

We want your tools and your little employees to be right back in their places so we need them, they are right there ready to work, and we want a spic and span workspace so we are less stressed and feel supported.

So you have sorted, and set in order, and shined, and now you move to your 4th S – standardize.

STANDARDIZE

The 4th S is –standardize.

Your rule here is what you practice, you become.

And your question is

How can I do this the same time every time?

Standardize is where the rubber meets the road, if you will.

Here is where all of the sorting, and setting in order and shining is finally paying off!

Here is where your space has been transformed into a streamlined, stress free place of life, and growth, and profit.

STANDARDIZE - WHAT YOU PRACTICE YOU BECOME!

Standardize: what you practice, you become!

You have made it simple and automatic for you to clean as you go and your space now respects you and your time and supports you.

Here is where you get your time back because it is all automatic, and has become a natural movement. You no longer have to stop and think about it, you just do it.

Your workspace is now automatically organized in the same exact way all the time. Your tools, your little employees are ready to do what you need them to do when you need them to.

Standardize is where you could have a 6 year old come in the workspace and you could walk them through what your particular process is step by step with everything that they would need to complete the task right there where they needed it to be and where it made sense for it to be.

Again, in Lean Six Sigma we want consistent purity, consistent quality. No variation!

And the great thing about this is that by the time you hit standardize, you have removed all sources of possible variation within your process, so if something does goes wrong, you will know immediately what is off, or what is different.

Also, if you find that you are doing the same thing every time you can ask yourself how best to standardize – **how can I do this the same way in the same time at the same level of quality without having to really think about it?**

A good rule of thumb is –

If I have done this twice in the past week then I need to automate this or make it a process.

❖ **What can I automate?**

You know things like can I make a template of this email that I send out saying the same thing over and over and other things like can I make a checklist so I don't have to worry about forgetting something?

Again, you have totally transformed your workspace by sorting what you use and what you don't, and setting your tools and little employees in order and shining up your workspace and created standard ways of doing things and keeping things.

So now that you have transformed your workspace let's keep it that way. And we are going to keep it that way with your last s – the 5th S.

SUSTAIN

The 5th S is Sustain

Your rule here is Maintain.

And your question is

How can I keep this space just like this all the time?

Here is where you have a new system that is easy to maintain because it is the most natural movement and flow for you.

You now want to put in a system that will help you to maintain your transformation.

Sustain – Maintain!

Sustain: Maintain!

I suggest that you create a checklist, a daily audit list and use it for at least three weeks until it becomes a natural habit for you.

You sorted and set in order and shined and standardized, so now you want to make it natural for you to continuously improve your process and your workspace because you look at the end of each day and go through and check off that you completed your tasks.

You also want to ask

- ❖ **What is working?**

- ❖ **What is not working?**

- ❖ **What is most important to me?**

You want daily review and daily clean up.

And remember your inventory list? Here is where you replenish Inventory - at end of day.

Think of a Sustain and a brand new way to end your day. A ritual if you will, to end your day with dignity.

You can review your workspace and make sure that all your tools and little employees are ready for another day tomorrow.

You can now switch gears and relax and enjoy your evening because you did exactly what you needed to do and will not have to worry if your forgot something.

Again the 5S are so simple and you want to keep this all super simple.

On my webpage is a free sample 5S Worksheet that you can download a copy of for you to adjust for yourself to help get you started!

Find it on my website at www.icfci.org

Transformation

Continuous Improvement is not a destination or an end to itself; it is a new path and a gateway to achieving your higher goals.

I want to challenge you to make your process flow so that is like a river, and the flow of it is just the most natural thing in the world!

Make it so that it becomes second nature to you and you can do it without even thinking about it — can you make it involuntary like breathing?

Process Improvement is about taking care of yourselves, and not punishing yourselves, so you must develop a system to reward excellence and make it a natural fluid movement, just like your value stream.

Transformation

- Define opportunity: 5 Whys
- Measure Performance: Value Stream Maps
- Analyze Opportunity: Is this Value Added or not?
- Improve Performance: 5S Your Workspace
- Control Performance: Make it Natural!

Transformation begins when you get honest with yourselves and admit there is a problem and you drill down into to it to clearly define it so you can look at it and measure your process and your workspace area and say here is where I am at currently, but here is where I want to be.

You map it out and begin to analyze each and every step so you can answer for yourself

Is this necessary?

And if it is, could I do it differently?

You get creative and begin to tweak things here and there to improve the flows of your workspace, your process, your workday so you can take back your time and your personal power!

You then develop a control system so that is honoring to yourself and your time.

JUMP BACK AND **KISS** MYSELF!

Kiss: Keep It Super Simple!

This is one of my favorite things to say –

KISS – Keep it Super Simple!

My Mentor taught me that the best proof of someone's intelligence is their ability to simplify the complex...

He also taught me that many of the world's most difficult problems have been solved with the simplest solutions.

Albert Einstein said "If you can't explain it to a six year old, you don't understand it yourself."

I love that!

So, are we working smarter and not harder?

This is how you want to run your process and your workspace and how it figure out if your solution is a smart one:

Is it simple?

Can it be easily explained?

Can it become a natural movement?

Again, there are no hard and fast rules here – this is about you figuring out what works best for you.

And keep it super simple, it is not complicated and it is not about a talent, this is a learned skill.

This is not about neatness; this is about a system, and designing a system that works for you.

You want happy environments that support you, who you are, and what you do.

Again, you want to simply streamline processes and workspaces that reflect who you are, what you want, and where you are going.

I LOVE ME!

I ♥ ME

- Self Love
- Self Respect
- Self Care
- Self Sufficiency
- Self Acceptance

You know what is so funny to me?

That Lean Six Sigma has so many 5's! 5 Whys and 5 S...

So I want to add a 6 S and My 6 S is Self-Care!

Again, to me, Lean Six Sigma is not about discipline it is all about self-care.

It is not a talent, it is a learned skill.

We use this tool to transform your process and your workspaces, and by doing that we transform yourselves - We use Lean Six Sigma to take your time back and your power back.

You have this time, this time in your day, and less stress, but this is extra time, time that you found and you took back for yourself.

This is not extra time for your workspace, or for your clients, no, this is time for you.

You are doing you this for you, to help you take care of you, for you to empower yourself and for you to give yourself self-love and self-respect, so please do something special just for you.

I want to encourage you, motivate you, and ignite your passion for yourself!

Let's make a list of your favorite things:

Here are a few of my Favorite Things…

Hobby:
Person:
Animal:
Food:
Drink:
Snack:
Shape:
Number:

Color:
Day:
Movie:
Song:
TV Show:
Game:
Season:
Month:
Book:
Fruit:
Vegetable:
Candy:
Place:

Is there something on your list that can be a catalyst for self care?

- ❖ **I'd really like to do:**

- ❖ **I'd really like to see:**

- ❖ **I'd really like to buy:**

- ❖ I'd really like my day to start with:

- ❖ I'd really like for my day to end with:

Please practice self-care and set up a reward system for yourself, whether it is a new pen or water bottle or pretty coffee mug or just a few moments of silent meditation or prayer…

Little Wins set the stage for Big Wins!

Let the outward transformation of your workspace begin an inner transformation!

NEED SOME HELP?

Questions?

Find Caroline online at www.icfci.org

Thank you for being with me on this adventure, and thank you for bringing your time, and your energy, and your focus.

On my website, the International Center for Continuous Improvement, I am adding templates, guides and resources for you to help you with your transformation - www.icfci.org.

There are so many free tools and tips online, but as I find good links, I promise you that I will post them! And if you need help with something, please feel free to email me and I'll be happy to help you and if I cannot do it, I'll really do my best to help find someone who can!

Blessings to each and every one of you as you transform your workspace, your life, and yourself!

Meet Caroline

Caroline is a Certified Lean Six Sigma Black Belt who specializes in coaching others in their homes, farms, classrooms, boardrooms, offices, assembly lines, organizations, and corporations how to increase productivity, increase quality, and increase income.

Caroline's mission is to help you see and then experience the possibility of greatness within your processes, yourself, and your office!

Caroline Bailey, LSSBB PMP, is a Process Improvement Specialist who specializes in coaching others in their homes, farms, classrooms, boardrooms, workspaces, assembly lines, organizations, and corporations how to increase productivity, increase quality, and increase income.

Caroline is a Certified Lean Sigma Black Belt through North Carolina State University and a Project Manager Professional certified through the Project Management Institute.

Caroline is the Founder and Executive Director of the International Center for Continuous Improvement, and is dedicated to helping others see and then experience the possibility of greatness within their processes, themselves, and their organizations.

www.ingramcontent.com/pod-product-compliance
Lightning Source LLC
Chambersburg PA
CBHW070332190526
45169CB00005B/1852